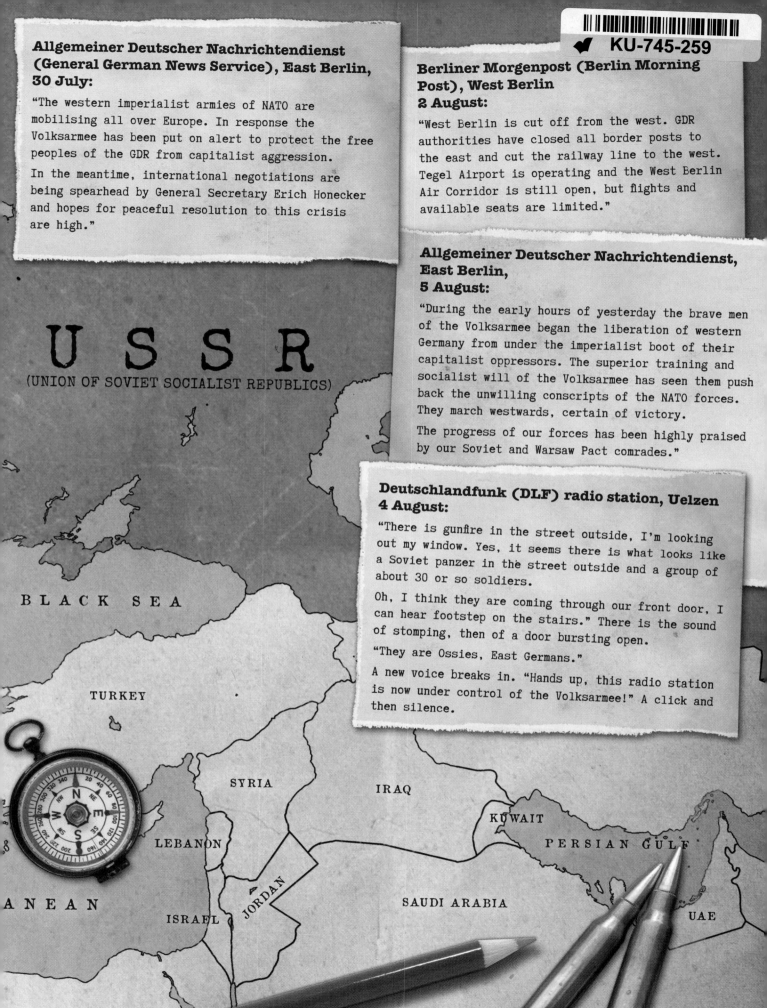

Allgemeiner Deutscher Nachrichtendienst (General German News Service), East Berlin, 30 July:

"The western imperialist armies of NATO are mobilising all over Europe. In response the Volksarmee has been put on alert to protect the free peoples of the GDR from capitalist aggression.

In the meantime, international negotiations are being spearhead by General Secretary Erich Honecker and hopes for peaceful resolution to this crisis are high."

Berliner Morgenpost (Berlin Morning Post), West Berlin 2 August:

"West Berlin is cut off from the west. GDR authorities have closed all border posts to the east and cut the railway line to the west. Tegel Airport is operating and the West Berlin Air Corridor is still open, but flights and available seats are limited."

Allgemeiner Deutscher Nachrichtendienst, East Berlin, 5 August:

"During the early hours of yesterday the brave men of the Volksarmee began the liberation of western Germany from under the imperialist boot of their capitalist oppressors. The superior training and socialist will of the Volksarmee has seen them push back the unwilling conscripts of the NATO forces. They march westwards, certain of victory.

The progress of our forces has been highly praised by our Soviet and Warsaw Pact comrades."

Deutschlandfunk (DLF) radio station, Uelzen 4 August:

"There is gunfire in the street outside, I'm looking out my window. Yes, it seems there is what looks like a Soviet panzer in the street outside and a group of about 30 or so soldiers.

Oh, I think they are coming through our front door, I can hear footstep on the stairs." There is the sound of stomping, then of a door bursting open.

"They are Ossies, East Germans."

A new voice breaks in. "Hands up, this radio station is now under control of the Volksarmee!" A click and then silence.

U S S R
(UNION OF SOVIET SOCIALIST REPUBLICS)

BLACK SEA

TURKEY

SYRIA

IRAQ

KUWAIT

PERSIAN GULF

LEBANON

JORDAN

SAUDI ARABIA

UAE

ISRAEL

ANEAN

EGYPT

IT'S 1985 AND THE COLD WAR JUST GOT HOT!

Team Yankee is a complete set of rules for playing World War III Wargames.

Based on the book written by Harold Coyle in 1987, Team Yankee brings the conflict that simmered throughout the Cold War to life. You will command your troops in miniature on a realistic battlefield.

In Team Yankee, a heavy combat team of M1 Abrams tanks and M113 armoured personnel carriers faces a Soviet invasion of West Germany. Outnumbered and outgunned, Captain Sean Bannon and his men will have to fight hard and they'll have to fight smart if they are going to survive.

Lt. Colonel Yuri Potecknov's motor rifle battalion is preparing to execute its mission in the scientific manner that he had been taught at the Frunze Military Academy and used in Afghanistan. Victory today will bring the world proletarian revolution that much closer.

Find out more at:

www.TEAM-YANKEE.com

© Copyright Battlefront Miniatures Ltd., 2016. ISBN: 9780992251635

VOLKS ARMEE
EAST GERMANS IN WORLD WAR III

Written by: Phil Yates and Wayne Turner

Editors: Peter Simunovich, John-Paul Brisigotti

Graphic Design: Casey Davies, Sean Goodison

Proof Readers: David Adlam, Chris Allen, Eis Annavini, Andrea Brischi, Alexander Costantino, Nick Faryna, Mark Goddard, Tim Harris, Mitch Kemmis, Paul Kitchin, Shane Kua, Mitchell Landrum, Michael McSwiney, Luke Parsonage, Gregg Siter, Stephen Smith, Luca Solvesi, Ryan Sullivan, Gavin van Rossum, Garry Wait, Daniel Wilson, Mark Wong

Miniatures Design: Evan Allen, Tim Adcock, Will Jayne

Cover Art and Illustrations: Vincent Wai

Miniatures Painting: Aaron Mathie

Web Support: James Brown

Playtest Groups: Dad's Army (Gavin Van Rossum), Northern Battle Gamers (Nigel Slater), Cavalieri dell'Esagono (Eis Annavini), Historical Tabletop Gaming Society (Shane Kua), The Yanks (Mitchell Landrum), with additional games from Maus Haus (Daniel Wilson), M.E.G. Team Voghera (Emilio Arbasino)

CONTENTS

NATIONALE VOLKSARMEE

THE GERMAN DEMOCRATIC REPUBLIC

After its defeat in the Second World War, Germany was occupied by the victorious Allied Powers. The Soviet Union controlled the part to the east of the Elbe River, while Britain, France and the United States occupied the part to the west.

In 1949, the separation of Germany was formalised with the creation of the Communist *Deutsche Demokratische Republik* (German Democratic Republic, East Germany) with its capital in East Berlin, and the pro-Western *Bundesrepublik Deutschland* (Federal German Republic, West Germany). Both republics claimed to be the legitimate government of the whole of Germany, not even recognising each other's existence until the 1970s.

The East Germany's path to statehood was not always smooth. Hundreds of thousands of Germans fled to the west before the border was closed in 1952. Then, in 1953, amidst post-war shortages, a strike over work quotas quickly spread to a nation-wide protest. The Communist government, fearing a counter-revolution, called in the Soviet Army to restore order. These disturbances left the Soviet leadership suspicious of the German Democratic Republic's loyalty and concerned about the power of a reunited Germany.

THE NATIONAL PEOPLE'S ARMY

Both East and West Germany established their post-war armed forces in 1956, with East Germany forming the *Nationale Volksarmee* (*NVA*, National People's Army).

Like West Germany's *Bundeswehr*, the leadership of the NVA was initially composed of soldiers who had served in the *Wehrmacht* under Nazi Germany. As soon as replacements loyal to the new regime could be trained, the *Wehrmacht* soldiers were retired. Despite their short period of leadership, they left a lasting legacy as the NVA combined Communist ideology with older German traditions.

The *Nationale Volksarmee* uniforms were a traditional stone grey rather than the Soviet khaki, while the helmets were subtly different, being based on a German design from 1945. Ranks, insignia, and other details followed traditional German forms as well.

The strong core of professional officers and non-commissioned officers was another traditional feature of German armed forces. Although most of the rank and file were short-service conscripts, half of the army were long-service professionals. This contrasts with the Soviet Army where only the officers were professionals, and particularly in combat units, non-commissioned officers were usually selected from amongst each batch of conscripts.

Despite the suspicions of the Soviet leadership, the NVA was staunchly loyal to the Communist regime. When Czechoslovak reforms went too far, the NVA prepared to invade the country along with their Soviet allies. Concerns over international opinion about German troops serving outside Germany limited their assistance to supporting roles.

Likewise in 1981, the NVA prepared to assist the Soviet Army in re-establishing order in Poland, though this was not needed when the Polish government declared martial law.

ORGANISATION AND EQUIPMENT

Like the rest of the Warsaw Pact armed forces, the NVA followed Soviet doctrine and organisation. Their two *Panzer* (tank) divisions and nine *Motorisierte Schützen* (motorised rifle) divisions were essentially similar to those of the Soviet army, although their equipment tended to be older, with relatively little of the very latest equipment.

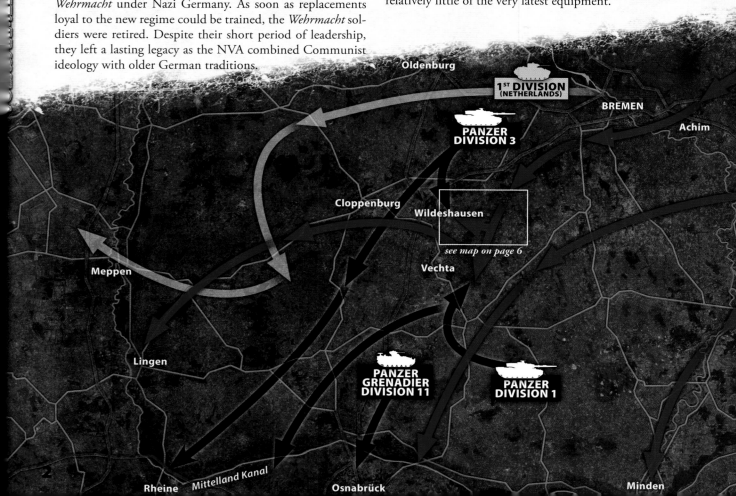

see map on page 6

9. PANZER DIVISION MOBILISES

As the Warsaw Pact prepared for war, *9. Panzer Division* mobilised and relocated by rail from their barracks at Eggesin to Potsdam (near Berlin) to join the Soviet Third Shock Army (headquartered at Magdeburg). They were included as one of the five tank divisions of the Third Shock Army. The army's orders were to punch through the NATO defences on the inner German border and push towards Bremen. In anticipation of the attack, *9. Panzer Division* made its way from Potsdam to the frontier with West Germany near Salzwedel.

9. Panzer Division was the pride of the NVA's armoured forces, equipped with the latest Soviet technology including T-72 tanks, BMP-1 and BMP-2 infantry fighting vehicles, and upgraded T-55AM2 tanks. They were the best trained troops in the Warsaw Pact with a higher proportion of full-time regular soldiers than their Soviet comrades. They had practiced and drilled for the eventuality of war, perfecting their offensive manoeuvres during Warsaw Pact exercises. The liberation of Germany awaited them.

On 4 August 1985 the Soviet 3rd Shock Army pushed across the inner German border and *9. Panzer Division* punched through the picket of the West German *Panzergrenadierdivision 11* around Bad Bevensen. Their T-72 and T-55AM2 tanks made short work of the defenders, a few Marder IFVs and Leopard 1 tanks. They then pushed on to the small town of Amelinghausen, before crossing Autobahn 7 at Bispingen.

As the division advanced across the North German Plain on those first two days, they continued to run into isolated pockets of NATO forces that had been bypassed by the advancing Soviet 10th Guards Tank Division to their south. They fought hard to cut through these localised remnants, as various units of exhausted West German and Dutch troops made desperate stands and ambushes, exacting a high price for every last centimetre of land.

It was just a few hours after crossing Autobahn 7 that they encountered freshly committed Dutch troops east of Bremen. An attack by Soviet airborne troops had already been fought off by the Dutch and West Germans by the time a concerted effort by the Soviet 20th Guards Army and 2nd Guards Tank Army to take Bremen began on 9 August, with *9. Panzer Division* joining the attack. Fighting was bitter and protracted as the Dutch Leopard tanks took their toll on the attacking Warsaw Pact tanks. After two days of fighting, the Soviet and East German superiority in infantry numbers finally told, and the Dutch were forced to withdraw.

As the Soviet 3rd Shock Army concentrated further south to break the British 1st Corps, *9. Panzer Division* was reassigned to the Soviet 20th Guards Army, where it joined the *Nationale Volksarmee 11. Motorisiertes Schützen Division* (11th Motorised Rifle Division) for the push south towards Osnabrück, Rheine, and the Mittelland Kanal.

VOLKSARMEE IN WORLD WAR III

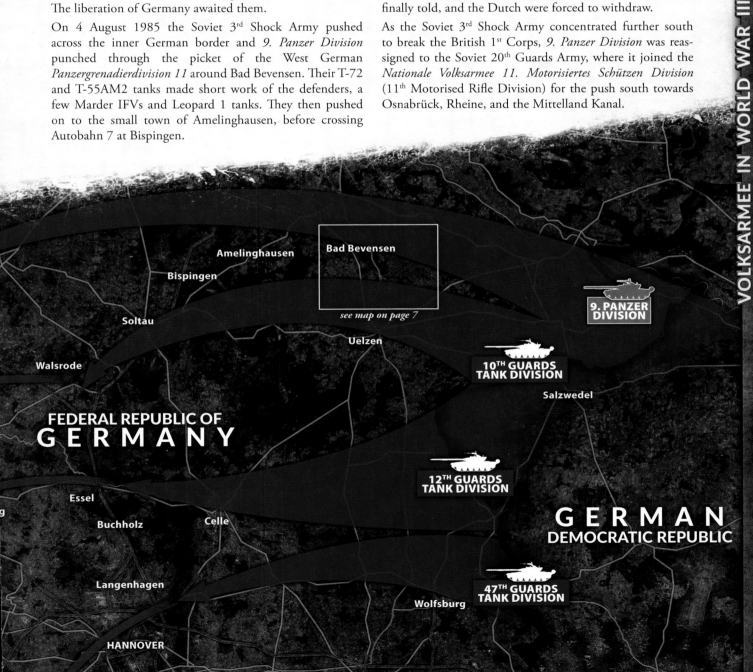

see map on page 7

FEDERAL REPUBLIC OF
GERMANY

GERMAN
DEMOCRATIC REPUBLIC

Again they faced more of their fellow Germans from the Bundeswehr, who conducted a stubborn fighting withdrawal toward the canal. A savage tank battle broke out around the town of Vechta as *9. Panzer Division* ran into the armoured rear guard of the West German *Panzerdivision 3*. Casualties were high on both sides, but eventually, night fell, and the West Germans continued their retreat under the cover of darkness.

By 12 August NATO had established a new defensive line behind the Mittelland Kanal. By this time *9. Panzer Division* was in need of replacements in both men and equipment, a pause in the fighting was taken to regroup and prepare for the next drive. Luckily, the socialist workers had not been idle and ammunition and replacement equipment had been brought up to depots established behind the front lines.

A day later *9. Panzer Division* was back in action, joining the 20th Guards Army's thrust farther west towards the Netherlands. They crossed the Dortmund-Elms Kanal at Lingen, after it had been taken by a helicopter borne assault the previous day. Soviet engineers had worked through the night to repair the bridges. Soviet and East German tanks

and armoured fighting vehicles streamed across the bridges and westward into the Netherlands. *9. Panzer Division* quickly faced a running defence from the Dutch, who had been recently reinforced by the British 2nd Corps. The Dutch took full advantage of the busy Dutch countryside, but superior training and careful reconnaissance made sure the East Germans did not fall into any cunning Dutch ambushes. By the end of 14 August, *9. Panzer Division* had taken the historic town of Arnhem.

The following day NATO launched a massive counterattack from their positions behind the Mittelland Kanal. The attack was made possible by the arrival of the US 3rd Corps. The forces of the Soviet 20th Guards Army and 2nd Guards Tank Army were forced to retreat. The next phase in *9. Panzer Division*'s war saw them counterattacking the flank of the NATO offensive against US and West German forces.

FRITZ'S WAR

'*Schlamperei* Ivan, sloppy', muttered *Oberleutnant* Fritz Fischer as he watched his *russische Kameraden* deploy from column to line. Two of the Russian tanks had been late in executing their turns and were racing to catch up their assigned positions, trailing clouds of diesel fumes. There was no way his men would ever be that sloppy.

They were Germans and proud of it. When it came to fighting the *Kapitalisten*, they would do it right, like a well-oiled machine, the way they had been trained. Liberating his German brothers in the West would unfortunately involve many casualties on both sides, but once the war was over the world would be a better place for everyone.

No time for thinking now, in a few moments it would be time for his *Panzer Kompanie* to advance. He raised his hand, then dropped it precisely on time. '*Panzers Vor!*' he spoke quietly over the radio. Moments later he was proud to see his ten T-72M tanks move off as one.

His tank rocked as it raced across the familiar training ground. 'Soon' he thought, 'soon we will be fighting for real. Soon we will have a chance to show these Russians how to fight, and perhaps, once Germany is whole again, it will have a chance to become great again, leading the proletariat of the world in their struggle.'

As Marx once said '*Macht und Freiheit sind identisch*' — Power and Freedom are identical.

2ND GUARDS TANK ARMY

20TH GUARDS ARMY

Mittelland Kanal

Osnabrück

Dortmund-Ems Kanal

Münster

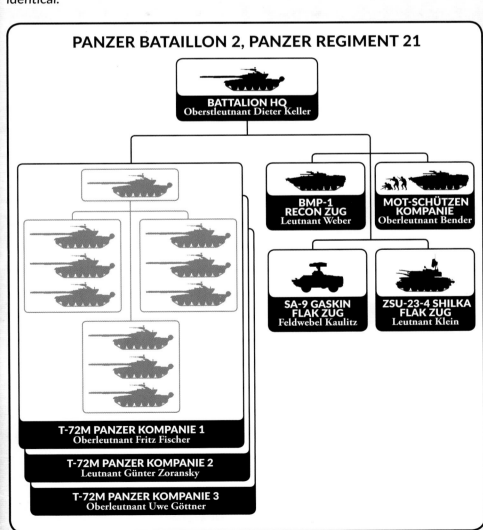

PANZER BATAILLON 2, PANZER REGIMENT 21

BATTALION HQ
Oberstleutnant Dieter Keller

BMP-1 RECON ZUG
Leutnant Weber

MOT-SCHÜTZEN KOMPANIE
Oberleutnant Bender

SA-9 GASKIN FLAK ZUG
Feldwebel Kaulitz

ZSU-23-4 SHILKA FLAK ZUG
Leutnant Klein

T-72M PANZER KOMPANIE 1
Oberleutnant Fritz Fischer

T-72M PANZER KOMPANIE 2
Leutnant Günter Zoransky

T-72M PANZER KOMPANIE 3
Oberleutnant Uwe Göttner

BAD BEVENSEN

Oberleutnant Fritz Fischer's company of T-72M panzers had been leading the battalion's advance since the early hours, encountering sporadic resistance as they advanced from the border towards their initial objective of Bremen. It was well past midday when they arrived at the small village of Groß Hesebeck, less then a kilometre from several key crossings over the Elbe-Seiten Canal. Beyond the canal lay the town of Bad Bevensen.

Fischer gathered with the battalion's other officers at the local *Gasthaus* (Inn) in Groß Hesebeck, where the battalion commander had set up his headquarters. He listened attentively as his commander out-lined the attack plan. Fischer's panzer company, along with the motor rifle company of Oberleutnant Bender, would attack from the village of Klein Hesebeck to the south towards Klein Bünstorf, crossing under the canal where it bridged the Ilmenau River and two local roads.

With the meeting dismissed and orders received, Fischer rushed back to his company and gave the order to move out. His panzers travelled south down the road to Klein Hesebeck before turning west towards the canal where engineers had erected several assault bridge across the narrow river. Bender's BMPs followed behind.

Fischer checked his watch and at 1315 hours, as planned, a barrage of rocket fire began to drop on the area immediately west of the canal bridge. As the barrage ended and a cloud of dust wafted above the canal, Fischer signalled his company to attack with a wave of his hand.

The T-72s rumbled forwards with a burst of diesel smoke, with a BMP-1 Aufklärungs Zug scouting ahead. The BMP scouts quickly disappeared into the dust billowing from the canal underpass. Fischer pushed his company forward with the lead panzers disappearing into the quickly dissipating smoke of the underpass. Fischer was the third tank through and was greeted with a volley of fire from the direction of Klein Bünstorf. The T-72 panzers quickly fanned out from the defile of the underpass and rumbled towards the village, and poured machine-gun and main gun fire towards it. Their fire was greeted with an occasional explosion from the edge of the village.

Fischer was suddenly distracted when one of his panzers exploded to his right. He quickly redirected his attention to the new threat, swinging his turret to the right and ordering his gunner to engage. His quick action was rewarded by an explosion in the tree line, and a smoking Wessi Leopard 1 rolled out into the field before halting as its crew bailed out and ran to safety.

After that, things quickly calmed down and the Wessies broke off, like they had done half-a-dozen times already that day, retiring to a new position. Fischer, had no time to admire his handy work, he had an objective to achieve. The city of Bremen awaited him. He pushed on beyond Klein Bünstorf and headed southwest to avoid the dense forest that loomed before him. Behind him Bender went about liberating the village and clearing out any last Wessi stragglers. To the north and south the rest of the division fought their way across the canal, eager to push west.

ADVANCING ON VECHTA

Having quickly pushed through a Dutch defensive position south of Bremen, Fischer's Panzer Kompanie headed southwest along Highway 51, before taking local roads towards Wildeshausen. Panzer Regiment 21 once more left the clearing of the town to the following BTR-60 mounted motor riflemen and their supporting T-55AM2 tanks, and skirted Wildeshausen to head towards Vechta.

As Fischer rode along in his tank with his head out of his commander's hatch, he peered into the distance. Shortly after passing through the small town of Goldenstedt, some movement in the distance caught his eye, vehicles, likely tanks, moving across a field. As Fischer's company was in the vanguard of the division it seemed unlikely that the vehicles were East German, and their Soviet Comrades were not meant to be in this area. He pondered for a moment, before coming to a decision. He quickly got on his radio and reported the unknown vehicles north of Vechta.

The regimental orders quickly returned back, 'Prepare to engage, and advance.' Fischer quickly organised his company into a line-abreast and began to move towards the enemy. To his right and left the rest of the battalion begun to spread out, with Bender's BMP Motor Rifle Company following behind once again. Before them, BMP-1 scouts probed ahead.

A 'crack' and the sudden eruption of flames from one of the BMPs shifted Fritz's attention to the large wood off to his right. "Achtung Panzer nach rechts!!" Fischer alerted his company to the location of the enemy. His company's tanks all quickly swung their turrets to the right. Another flash from the wood's edge pinpointed another enemy tank and Fischer ordered his tanks to fire. A fusillade of 125mm gun fire fol-

lowed and the edge of the wood erupted in flame, dust, and shattered tree limbs.

Fischer's tanks continued to roll forward, redirecting their movement towards the wood, while firing on its edge. More fire came their way and one of Fischer's tanks went up in flames, swiftly followed by several others from the battalion's other companies. With the rest of the battalion's tanks joining the fire fight, more explosions soon erupted from the wood's edge. As the T-72M tanks closed to within 400 metres of the wood, Bender's riflemen passed through them and approached to within 200 metres before dismounting their BMP-1 infantry fighting vehicles. The motor riflemen then rapidly advanced on the wood, firing their assault rifles as they moved forward. Their assault was met with only light fire, due to the suppressive fire laid down by the T-72Ms and BMP-1s.

Oberleutnant Bender soon reported back on the captured two immobilised Leopard 2 tanks, but the rest of the West Germans had withdrawn. While the riflemen continued to clear the wood, Fischer's company pushed southwest past the village of Lutten. Spread out before Fischer, about two kilometres distant, was the small city of Vechta. While Fischer looked ahead, searching the terrain for signs of the enemy, a crash and boom brought his attention back to his immediate surroundings. An enemy artillery barrage had begun falling around his company. He quickly ducked back into the turret and closed his hatch.

Fischer ordered his company to keep moving, while the rattle and thump of shrapnel, dirt, and rocks hitting reverberated around his tank. His company eventually pushed beyond the area of the barrage. The two remaining BMP scouts shot out ahead of the battalion, searching for the next enemy position.

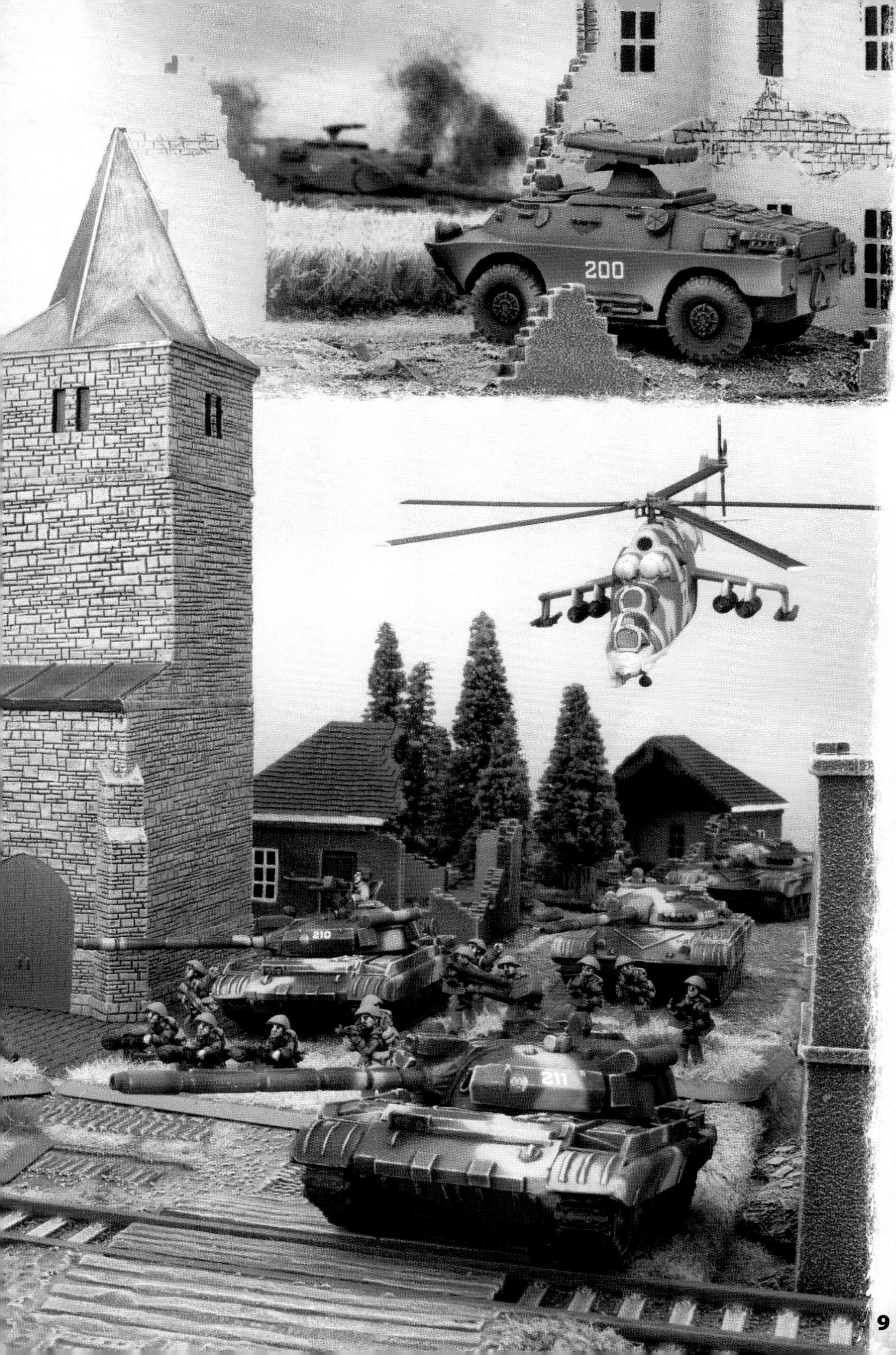
200
210
211

9. PANZER DIVISION

As Oberleutnant Fritz Fischer's T-72 tanks approached the outskirts of the Dutch town of Rijssen he called a halt and stopped behind a tree line marking the boundary of a field. He climbed out of his turret and made his way to the tree line with his binoculars. A few minutes later he was joined by his good friend Oberleutnant Dieter Bender, who's BMP-1 mounted riflemen were following Fritz's company, and the commander of the BMP scouts, Leutnant Weber.

"What do you see?' asked Bender.

"Nothing yet, I thought I saw some movement to the left, but no more as yet." Fritz responded, before outlining his thinking. "I think we should swing around to the right of the town, go through the industrial area where it is more open and the Dutch have less concealment."

Bender and Weber nodded in agreement. After returning to his tank, Fritz gained quick approval for his plan from the battalion headquarters, and ten minutes later the formation was underway again, with Weber's scouts racing ahead.

The line of T-72s burst through the tree line and headed to the right, cutting across fields before entering wide streets lined with warehouses, factories, and workshops. Bender's men had dismounted, escorting the tanks as they moved cautiously through the industrial parkland, while the scouts covered the left flank.

A glint of sunlight caught Fritz's eye as he peered forward from his cupola's vision blocks. As he searched to find what it was, the adjacent T-72 rocked and was enveloped in a cloud of dust. He quickly spied a tank off in the distance, amongst some silos.

"Panzer, silos" he barked to his gunner.

His gunner quickly acquired the target and returned with a range, "1300 metres".

"Feuer frei!" he ordered and his gunner sent a round towards the target.

In the distance there was a burst of flame and dust. Fritz watched as the Dutch crew scrambled out of their Leopard 1 tank.

"Stay alert," he called over the radio to his company, "there are bound to be more."

The previous Minister of National Defence, Heinz Hoffmann, was a veteran of the Spanish Civil War, and was honoured after his death when the best equipped formation in the NVA was retitled 9. *Panzer Division 'Heinz Hoffmann'*.

The division had been entirely equipped with T-72M tanks, having none of the T-55AM2 tanks found in other divisions. In addition, two of its motor rifle battalions had one of their companies equipped with the latest BMP-2 infantry fighting vehicles, the only examples of this powerful weapon in the entire NVA.

Aside from their tanks and infantry fighting vehicles, the remaining weapons were much the same as any Soviet division, with 2S1 Carnation self-propelled howitzers in the artillery battalions, BM-21 Hail rocket launchers in the rocket battalion, and Mi-24 Hind helicopter gunships in the combat helicopter squadrons.

As the likelihood of war became more apparent, the East Germans further reinforced 9. *Panzer Division* with a *motorisietes schützen regiment* (motorised rifle regiment) from 8. *Motorisietes Schutzen Division*. This regiment was equipped with 8-wheeled BTR armoured transporters, which could take advantage of their superior speed in their breakthrough role, especially on the autobahn motorways of West Germany.

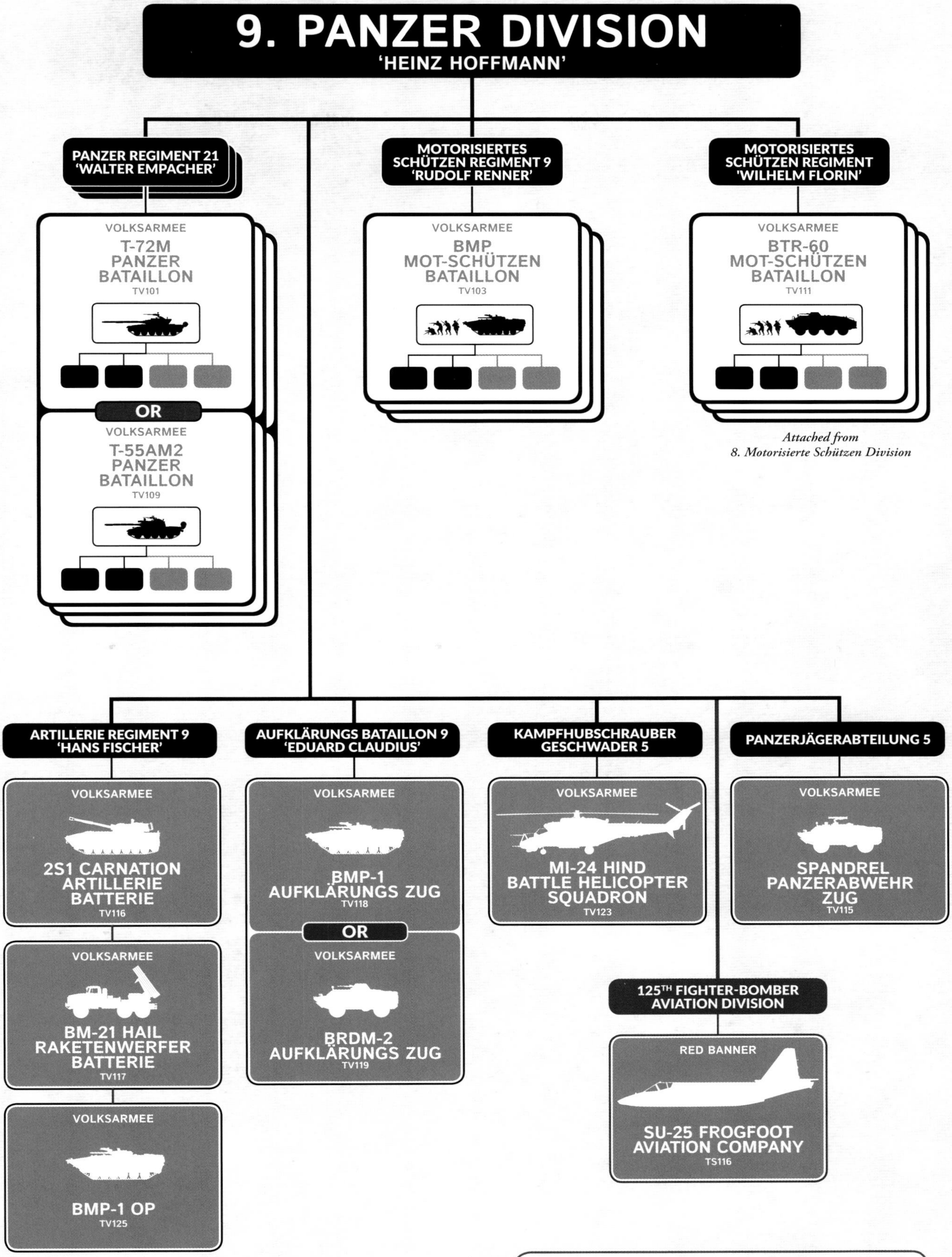

9. PANZER DIVISION
'HEINZ HOFFMANN'

PANZER REGIMENT 21 'WALTER EMPACHER'

VOLKSARMEE
T-72M PANZER BATAILLON
TV101

OR

VOLKSARMEE
T-55AM2 PANZER BATAILLON
TV109

MOTORISIERTES SCHÜTZEN REGIMENT 9 'RUDOLF RENNER'

VOLKSARMEE
BMP MOT-SCHÜTZEN BATAILLON
TV103

MOTORISIERTES SCHÜTZEN REGIMENT 'WILHELM FLORIN'

VOLKSARMEE
BTR-60 MOT-SCHÜTZEN BATAILLON
TV111

Attached from
8. Motorisierte Schützen Division

ARTILLERIE REGIMENT 9 'HANS FISCHER'

VOLKSARMEE
2S1 CARNATION ARTILLERIE BATTERIE
TV116

VOLKSARMEE
BM-21 HAIL RAKETENWERFER BATTERIE
TV117

VOLKSARMEE
BMP-1 OP
TV125

AUFKLÄRUNGS BATAILLON 9 'EDUARD CLAUDIUS'

VOLKSARMEE
BMP-1 AUFKLÄRUNGS ZUG
TV118

OR

VOLKSARMEE
BRDM-2 AUFKLÄRUNGS ZUG
TV119

KAMPFHUBSCHRAUBER GESCHWADER 5

VOLKSARMEE
MI-24 HIND BATTLE HELICOPTER SQUADRON
TV123

PANZERJÄGERABTEILUNG 5

VOLKSARMEE
SPANDREL PANZERABWEHR ZUG
TV115

125TH FIGHTER-BOMBER AVIATION DIVISION

RED BANNER
SU-25 FROGFOOT AVIATION COMPANY
TS116

> *9. Panzer Division* has three tank regiments, all named for famous Communists.
> - *Panzer Regiment 21* 'Walter Empacher'
> - *Panzer Regiment 22* 'Soja Kosmodemjanskaja'
> - *Panzer Regiment 23* 'Julian Marchlewski'

VOLKSARMEE

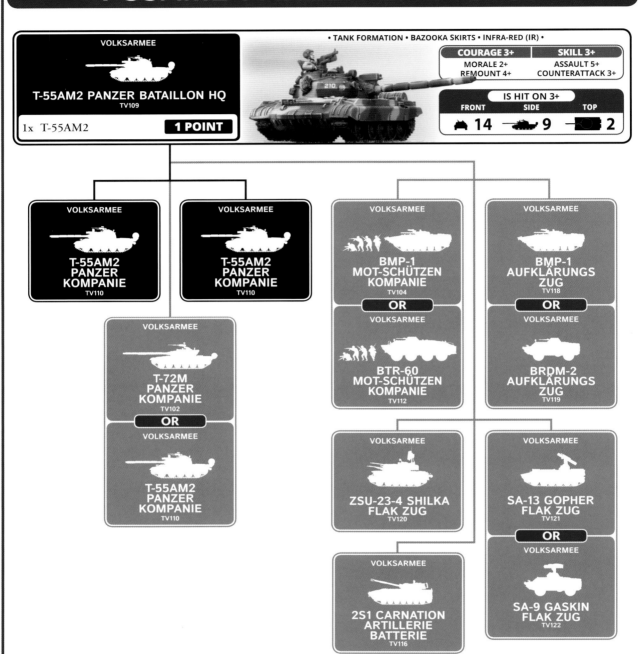

VOLKSARMEE
T-55AM2 PANZER BATAILLON

VOLKSARMEE
T-55AM2 PANZER BATAILLON HQ
TV109

1x T-55AM2 — **1 POINT**

• TANK FORMATION • BAZOOKA SKIRTS • INFRA-RED (IR) •

COURAGE 3+	SKILL 3+
MORALE 2+	ASSAULT 5+
REMOUNT 4+	COUNTERATTACK 3+

IS HIT ON 3+		
FRONT	SIDE	TOP
14	9	2

VOLKSARMEE
T-55AM2 PANZER KOMPANIE
TV110

VOLKSARMEE
T-55AM2 PANZER KOMPANIE
TV110

VOLKSARMEE
T-72M PANZER KOMPANIE
TV102

OR

VOLKSARMEE
T-55AM2 PANZER KOMPANIE
TV110

VOLKSARMEE
BMP-1 MOT-SCHÜTZEN KOMPANIE
TV104

OR

VOLKSARMEE
BTR-60 MOT-SCHÜTZEN KOMPANIE
TV112

VOLKSARMEE
BMP-1 AUFKLÄRUNGS ZUG
TV118

OR

VOLKSARMEE
BRDM-2 AUFKLÄRUNGS ZUG
TV119

VOLKSARMEE
ZSU-23-4 SHILKA FLAK ZUG
TV120

VOLKSARMEE
2S1 CARNATION ARTILLERIE BATTERIE
TV116

VOLKSARMEE
SA-13 GOPHER FLAK ZUG
TV121

OR

VOLKSARMEE
SA-9 GASKIN FLAK ZUG
TV122

VOLKSARMEE

His tank might have been older than he was, but *Unteroffizier* Meyer was proud of it nonetheless. That made his current predicament even more galling. He'd driven into the ditch at the side of the road and was stuck. Worse, he was blocking the road and he could feel the eyes of everyone behind him boring into the back of his head.

'*Dummkopf!*' he muttered to himself as he gestured to his driver to swing hard left.

With a clash of gears and cloud of diesel smoke, the T-55 tank eased itself out of the ditch and back onto the road. Meyer climbed back aboard, clambering over the 'eyebrows' on the front of the turret and swinging back into his position as the tank commander.

'Meyer, *sehen!*' His gunner's shout drew his eyes up from the road ahead as three *Wessi* Leopard tanks moved out from the village, positioning themselves to ambush the rest of the battalion as it continued its advance. They didn't seem to have seen him and the rest of the column stuck behind them.

Meyer smiled. His tank may be old, but it had the latest *technik* and the best crew.

'Range 985m'. His gunner's glee at getting to use the laser rangefinder against a real enemy tank was clear.

'Take the front one,' Meyer ordered. 'It'll confuse the other two.'

Switching to the platoon circuit, Meyer's curt '*Zu Leine!*' quickly had his other two tanks off the road and in line beside him. The *Wessies* wouldn't know what hit them!

VOLKSARMEE
T-55AM2 PANZER KOMPANIE

T-55AM2 PANZER KOMPANIE

10x T-55AM2	**16 POINTS**
9x T-55AM2	**14 POINTS**
8x T-55AM2	**12 POINTS**
7x T-55AM2	**10 POINTS**
6x T-55AM2	**8 POINTS**
5x T-55AM2	**6 POINTS**
4x T-55AM2	**4 POINTS**
3x T-55AM2	**2 POINTS**

OPTIONS
• Fit up to three T-55AM2 tanks with Mine Clearing Devices for +1 point.

Of the 2100 T-55 tanks supplied to NVA by the Soviet Union, Czechoslovakia, and Poland, nearly 300 were upgraded to the T-55AM2 standard.

The T-55AM2 was fitted with a modern fire control system with a ballistic calculator, calculating such things as air pressure, air temperature, weight of ammunition, reduced velocity for tube wear, and so on. It was also fitted with a laser rangefinder.

• TANK UNIT • BAZOOKA SKIRTS • INFRA-RED (IR) •

COURAGE 4+	SKILL 4+
MORALE 3+	ASSAULT 5+
REMOUNT 4+	COUNTERATTACK 4+

IS HIT ON 3+		
FRONT	SIDE	TOP
14	9	2

TACTICAL	TERRAIN DASH	CROSS COUNTRY DASH	ROAD DASH	CROSS
10"/25CM	14"/35CM	20"/50CM	24"/60CM	4+

WEAPON	RANGE	ROF HALTED	MOVING	ANTI-TANK	FIRE-POWER	NOTES
100mm D10-T gun	32"/80CM	1	1	17	2+	*Laser Rangefinder, Slow Firing*
12.7mm AA MG	20"/50CM	3	2	4	5+	
7.62mm MG	16"/40CM	1	1	2	6	

Crew: 4 - commander, gunner, loader, driver
Weight: 40.5 tonnes
Length: 9.00m (29' 6")
Width: 3.37m (11' 1")
Height: 2.40m (7' 10")

Weapons: 100mm D-10T gun
12.7mm NVST MG
7.62mm PKT MG
Armour: 203mm with add-on armour
Speed: 48 km/h (30 mph)
Engine: V-12 diesel 455 kW (620 hp)
Range: 740 km (460 miles)

VOLKSARMEE
T-72M PANZER BATAILLON

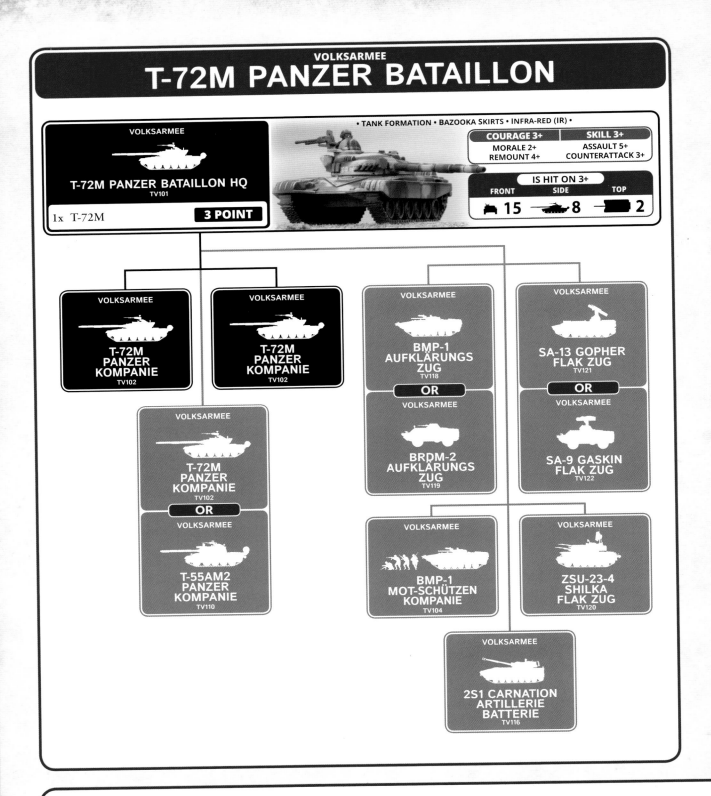

• TANK FORMATION • BAZOOKA SKIRTS • INFRA-RED (IR) •

VOLKSARMEE

T-72M PANZER BATAILLON HQ
TV101

1x T-72M — **3 POINT**

COURAGE 3+	SKILL 3+
MORALE 2+	ASSAULT 5+
REMOUNT 4+	COUNTERATTACK 3+

IS HIT ON 3+

FRONT	SIDE	TOP
15	8	2

VOLKSARMEE
T-72M PANZER KOMPANIE
TV102

VOLKSARMEE
T-72M PANZER KOMPANIE
TV102

VOLKSARMEE
T-72M PANZER KOMPANIE
TV102
OR
VOLKSARMEE
T-55AM2 PANZER KOMPANIE
TV110

VOLKSARMEE
BMP-1 AUFKLÄRUNGS ZUG
TV118
OR
VOLKSARMEE
BRDM-2 AUFKLÄRUNGS ZUG
TV119

VOLKSARMEE
SA-13 GOPHER FLAK ZUG
TV121
OR
VOLKSARMEE
SA-9 GASKIN FLAK ZUG
TV122

VOLKSARMEE
BMP-1 MOT-SCHÜTZEN KOMPANIE
TV104

VOLKSARMEE
ZSU-23-4 SHILKA FLAK ZUG
TV120

VOLKSARMEE
2S1 CARNATION ARTILLERIE BATTERIE
TV116

'*Panzers Vor!*' Oberleutnant Fischer's excitement was hard to hide, even over the radio. This was it. The moment he'd spent years training for. He was about to face the enemy for the first time.

With a rolling, moaning, ear-splitting howl, the rocket launchers behind filled the air with smoke trails. Moments later, the woods that hid the *Westdeutsche* seemed to rise into the air before disappearing in a cloud of smoke and dust as his tanks raced towards it. Surely nothing could remain of the *Wessies* after such a pounding.

The thought died along with three of his men when one of his panzers lost its cap, its turret flipping over and over as it spun though the air.

'*Achtung! Feuer Frei,*' Fischer ordered as more missiles began streaking from the clearing dust cloud. '*Schmidt, Sprenggranate, 800m, Feuer!*' he barked a fire order to his own gunner. The rattle of the autoloader was lost in the roar of the tank's diesel engine, but nothing could block out the crash of a 125mm gun as it fired.

VOLKSARMEE
T-72M PANZER KOMPANIE

• TANK UNIT • BAZOOKA SKIRTS • INFRA-RED (IR) •

T-72M PANZER KOMPANIE

10x	T-72M	**35 POINTS**
9x	T-72M	**31 POINTS**
8x	T-72M	**27 POINTS**
7x	T-72M	**23 POINTS**
6x	T-72M	**19 POINTS**
5x	T-72M	**15 POINTS**
4x	T-72M	**11 POINTS**
3x	T-72M	**7 POINTS**

OPTIONS
* Fit up to three T-72M tanks with Mine Clearing Devices for +1 point.

COURAGE 4+	SKILL 4+
MORALE 3+	ASSAULT 5+
REMOUNT 4+	COUNTERATTACK 4+

IS HIT ON 3+

FRONT	SIDE	TOP
15	8	2

TACTICAL	TERRAIN DASH	CROSS COUNTRY DASH	ROAD DASH	CROSS
10"/25CM	16"/40CM	24"/60CM	28"/70CM	3+

WEAPON	RANGE	ROF HALTED	ROF MOVING	ANTI-TANK	FIRE-POWER	NOTES
125mm 2A46 gun	32"/80CM	1	1	21	2+	Brutal, Laser Rangefinder, Stabiliser
12.7mm AA MG	20"/50CM	3	2	4	5+	
7.62mm MG	16"/40CM	1	1	2	6	

The T-72 tank is easy to build and simple to use, making it an ideal replacement for the older T-55 tank. Both Czechoslovakia and Poland produced the T-72M version of the T-72, and sold them widely, including to the *Nationale Volksarmee*.

The T-72M lacks some of the more technology of the Soviet-built T-72 tanks and is not equipped with the latest high-tech anti-tank ammunition. Despite this, it is still a big step forward for the NVA, being fast, accurate and deadly, even when moving at speed. Its autoloader replaces the fourth crew member, a significant improvement for a small army like the NVA, allowing it to operate with 25% less personnel in its panzer companies.

The highly-trained German crews know how to take advantage of its strengths and weaknesses, and how to combine its operations with supporting arms to overcome even the best NATO tanks, and expect little trouble dealing with older equipment.

Crew: 3 - commander, gunner, driver
Weight: 41 tonnes
Length: 9.50m (31'2")
Width: 3.50m (11'6")
Height: 2.20m (7'3")
Weapons: 125mm 2A46 gun
12.7mm NVST MG
7.62mm PKT MG
Armour: Composite 24cm RHA equivalent, 42cm against HEAT
Speed: 60 km/h (37 mph)
Engine: V-12 diesel 582 kW (780 hp)
Range: 700 km (430 miles)

BAZOOKA SKIRTS

The Czech-manufactured T-72M tanks of the *Volksarmee* did not have the BDD armour of the later model T-72 tanks used by the Soviets. To compensate for this, the T-72M was fitted with 'bazooka skirts', spaced armour to protect them from light, hand-held anti-tank weapons.

Teams with Bazooka Skirts have a Side armour rating of 10 against HEAT weapons.

'*Wieder*, 700m,' Fischer ordered another shot, the range closing quickly. His men were good, but the targets were hard to spot. There were explosions all along the tree line and the second volley of missiles was weaker than the first. '*Wieder*, 600m,' again, he ordered, the tank throwing him against his cupola sight as it rocked through a small ditch. His padded helmet took the blow, but he hardly noticed.

'*Kompanie, Halt!*' The tank rocked to a halt as the BMP *Schützenpanzers* raced past.

'*Achtsam Schmidt*', he bellowed, careful. Now wasn't the time for sloppiness, for a rushed shot to hit one of the BMP fighting vehicles dashing forward. Any moment now they too would stop and it would be an infantry fight.

BMP MOT-SCHÜTZEN BATAILLON

VOLKSARMEE

BMP MOT-SCHÜTZEN BATAILLON HQ
TV103

1x MPi KM team
1x BMP-1 (TV105)

1 POINT

• INFANTRY FORMATION • HQ TRANSPORT •

COURAGE 3+	SKILL 3+
MORALE 2+	ASSAULT 5+
RALLY 3+	COUNTERATTACK 3+

IS HIT ON	INFANTRY SAVE
3+	3+

TACTICAL	TERRAIN DASH	CROSS COUNTRY DASH	ROAD DASH	CROSS
8"/20CM	8"/20CM	12"/30CM	12"/30CM	AUTO

WEAPON	RANGE	ROF HALTED	ROF MOVING	ANTI-TANK	FIRE-POWER	NOTES
MPi KM assault rifle team	8"/20CM	3	3	1	6	Pinned ROF 1

VOLKSARMEE

BMP-1 MOT-SCHÜTZEN KOMPANIE
TV104

OR

VOLKSARMEE

BMP-2 MOT-SCHÜTZEN KOMPANIE
TV106

VOLKSARMEE

BMP-1 MOT-SCHÜTZEN KOMPANIE
TV104

VOLKSARMEE

BMP-1 MOT-SCHÜTZEN KOMPANIE
TV104

VOLKSARMEE

T-72M PANZER KOMPANIE
TV102

OR

VOLKSARMEE

T-55AM2 PANZER KOMPANIE
TV110

VOLKSARMEE

BMP-1 AUFKLÄRUNGS ZUG
TV118

OR

VOLKSARMEE

BRDM-2 AUFKLÄRUNGS ZUG
TV119

VOLKSARMEE

2S1 CARNATION ARTILLERIE BATTERIE
TV116

VOLKSARMEE

SPANDREL PANZERABWEHR ZUG
TV115

VOLKSARMEE

ZSU-23-4 SHILKA FLAK ZUG
TV120

VOLKSARMEE

SA-13 GOPHER FLAK ZUG
TV121

OR

VOLKSARMEE

SA-9 GASKIN FLAK ZUG
TV122

BMP-1 MOT-SCHÜTZEN KOMPANIE

BMP-1 MOT-SCHÜTZEN KOMPANIE

10x MPi KM team with RPG-18 anti-tank
9x RPG-7 anti-tank team
2x PKM LMG team
12x BMP-1 (TV105)   **19 POINTS**

7x MPi KM team with RPG-18 anti-tank
6x RPG-7 anti-tank team
2x PKM LMG team
9x BMP-1 (TV105)   **14 POINTS**

4x MPi KM team with RPG-18 anti-tank
3x RPG-7 anti-tank team
4x BMP-1 (TV105)   **6 POINTS**

OPTIONS
- Add AGS-17 grenade launcher team & BMP-1 for +1 point.
- Add SA-14 Gremlin AA missile team & BMP-1 for +1 point.

The Russian BMP-1 is the successor to Germany's ground-breaking Hanomag half-track of the Second World War. It carries the *Schützen* into battle in relative safety, then gives them fire support as they launch their attack.

Mounting an AT-3 Sagger missile, the BMP-1 also protects the infantry from enemy panzers.

The company's riflemen are armed with the classic AKM assault rifle, or *MPi KM (Maschinenpistole Kalashnikow Modernisiert)* submachine-gun as the East Germans called them. Each squad is also equipped with an RPK squad automatic weapon, disposable RPG-18 anti-tank rockets, and the powerful RPG-7 anti-tank rocket launcher.

The company is backed up by a platoon of six belt-fed PKM machine-guns, as well as AGS-17 30mm grenade launchers, all mounted in BMPs.

With the threat of war looming the companies have had their old *Strela-2* anti-aircraft missiles replaced with newer *Strela-3* (Arrow-3) aircraft missiles (known as *Strela-14* Gremlin in the West). These are deployed in a squad, mounted in another BMP, attached from the battalion's air defence platoon.

• INFANTRY UNIT •

COURAGE 4+	SKILL 4+
MORALE 3+	ASSAULT 5+
RALLY 4+	COUNTERATTACK 4+

IS HIT ON	INFANTRY SAVE
3+	3+

TACTICAL	TERRAIN DASH	CROSS COUNTRY DASH	ROAD DASH	CROSS
8"/20CM	8"/20CM	12"/30CM	12"/30CM	AUTO

WEAPON	RANGE	HALTED	MOVING	ANTI-TANK	FIRE-POWER	NOTES
MPi KM assault rifle team or RPG-18 anti-tank	8"/20CM 8"/20CM	3 1	3 1	1 14	6 5+	Pinned ROF 1 HEAT, Slow Firing
RPG-7 anti-tank team	12"/30CM	1	1	17	4+	Assault 6, HEAT, Slow Firing
PKM LMG team	16"/40CM	7	4	2	6	Assault 6, Heavy Weapon

WEAPONS CARD

The BMP-1 Motorisiertes Schützen Kompanie is a flexible unit with a wide variety of weapons from assault rifles to automatic grenade launchers. It has an additional card, [TV108], with the data for its heavy support weapons.

WEAPON	RANGE	ROF HALTED	MOVING	ANTI-TANK	FIRE-POWER	NOTES
AGS-17 grenade launcher team	16"/40CM	9	3	3	6	Assault 6, Heavy Weapon
SA-14 Gremlin AA missile team	48"/120CM	3	-	-	5+	Assault 6, Guided AA, Heavy Weapon

BMP-1 TRANSPORT

• TANK ATTACHMENT • AMPHIBIOUS • INFRA-RED (IR) • PASSENGERS 2 •

COURAGE 4+	SKILL 4+
MORALE 3+	ASSAULT 5+
REMOUNT 4+	COUNTERATTACK 4+

IS HIT ON 3+		
FRONT	SIDE	TOP
2	2	1

TACTICAL	TERRAIN DASH	CROSS COUNTRY DASH	ROAD DASH	CROSS
10"/25CM	16"/40CM	28"/70CM	32"/80CM	3+

WEAPON	RANGE	ROF HALTED	MOVING	ANTI-TANK	FIRE-POWER	NOTES
73mm 2A28 gun	16"/40CM	1	1	12	3+	HEAT
AT-3 Sagger missile	16"/40CM– 44"/110CM	1	-	19	3+	Guided, HEAT
7.62mm MG	16"/40CM	3	3	2	6	

Crew: 3 – commander, driver, gunner
Weight: 13 tonnes
Length: 6.74m (22' 1")
Width: 2.94m (9' 8")
Height: 1.92m (6' 3")

Weapons: 73mm 2A28 gun
AT-3 Sagger guided missile
7.62mm PKT MG
Armour: 33mm
Speed: 65 km/h (40 mph)
Range: 600 km (370 miles)

VOLKSARMEE
BMP-2 MOT-SCHÜTZEN KOMPANIE

BMP-2 MOT-SCHÜTZEN KOMPANIE	
10x MPi KM team with RPG-18 anti-tank	
9x RPG-7 anti-tank team	
2x PKM LMG team	
12x BMP-2 (TV107)	**24 POINTS**
7x MPi KM team with RPG-18 anti-tank	
6x RPG-7 anti-tank team	
2x PKM LMG team	
9x BMP-2 (TV107)	**18 POINTS**
4x MPi KM team with RPG-18 anti-tank	
3x RPG-7 anti-tank team	
4x BMP-2 (TV107)	**8 POINTS**

OPTIONS
- Add AGS-17 grenade launcher team & BMP-2 for +2 points.
- Add SA-14 Gremlin AA missile team & BMP-2 for +2 points.

Each *motorisiertes schützen regiment* in *9. Panzer Division* has one company of the new BMP-2. These new infantry fighting vehicles are armed with the latest weapons systems developed by the Soviets. They carry a powerful *Konkurs* (named AT-5 Spandrel by NATO) anti-tank missile, which is able to deal with more heavily armoured enemy tanks. The main turret is armed with a rapid-firing 30mm 2A42 automatic cannon, more than capable of destroying any NATO infantry fighting vehicle or other light armour they may encounter.

• INFANTRY UNIT •

COURAGE 4+	SKILL 4+
MORALE 3+ RALLY 4+	ASSAULT 5+ COUNTERATTACK 4+

IS HIT ON	INFANTRY SAVE
3+	**3+**

TACTICAL	TERRAIN DASH	CROSS COUNTRY DASH	ROAD DASH	CROSS
8"/20CM	8"/20CM	12"/30CM	12"/30CM	AUTO

WEAPON	RANGE	HALTED	MOVING	ANTI-TANK	FIRE-POWER	NOTES
MPi KM assault rifle team	8"/20CM	3	3	1	6	*Pinned ROF 1*
or RPG-18 anti-tank	8"/20CM	1	1	14	5+	*HEAT, Slow Firing*
RPG-7 anti-tank team	12"/30CM	1	1	17	4+	*Assault 6, HEAT, Slow Firing*
PKM LMG team	16"/40CM	7	4	2	6	*Assault 6, Heavy Weapon*

WEAPONS CARD

The BMP-2 Motorisiertes Schützen Kompanie is a flexible unit with a wide variety of weapons from assault rifles to automatic grenade launchers. It has an additional card, [TV108], with the data for its heavy support weapons.

WEAPON	RANGE	ROF HALTED	MOVING	ANTI-TANK	FIRE-POWER	NOTES
AGS-17 grenade launcher team	16"/40CM	9	3	3	6	*Assault 6, Heavy Weapon*
SA-14 Gremlin AA missile team	48"/120CM	3	-	-	5+	*Assault 6, Guided AA, Heavy Weapon*

VOLKSARMEE
BMP-2 TRANSPORT

• TANK ATTACHMENT • AMPHIBIOUS • INFRA-RED (IR) • PASSENGERS 2 •

COURAGE 4+	SKILL 4+
MORALE 3+ REMOUNT 4+	ASSAULT 5+ COUNTERATTACK 4+

IS HIT ON 3+

FRONT	SIDE	TOP
2	2	1

TACTICAL	TERRAIN DASH	CROSS COUNTRY DASH	ROAD DASH	CROSS
10"/25CM	16"/40CM	24"/60CM	32"/80CM	3+

WEAPON	RANGE	ROF HALTED	MOVING	ANTI-TANK	FIRE-POWER	NOTES
30mm 2A42 gun	20"/50CM	3	2	10	5+	*Anti-helicopter, Stabiliser*
AT-5 Spandrel missile	8"/20CM– 48"/120CM	1	-	21	3+	*Guided, HEAT*
7.62mm MG	16"/40CM	3	3	2	6	

BMP-1 AUFKLÄRUNGS ZUG

• TANK UNIT • AMPHIBIOUS • INFRA-RED (IR) • SPEARHEAD •

BMP-1 AUFKLÄRUNGS ZUG	
4x BMP-1 Scout	**4 POINTS**
3x BMP-1 Scout	**3 POINTS**
2x BMP-1 Scout	**2 POINTS**

COURAGE 4+	SKILL 4+
MORALE 3+	ASSAULT 5+
REMOUNT 4+	COUNTERATTACK 4+

IS HIT ON 3+

FRONT	SIDE	TOP
2	2	1

TACTICAL	TERRAIN DASH	CROSS COUNTRY DASH	ROAD DASH	CROSS
10"/25CM	16"/40CM	28"/70CM	32"/80CM	3+

WEAPON	RANGE	ROF HALTED	ROF MOVING	ANTI-TANK	FIRE-POWER	NOTES
73mm 2A28 gun	16"/40CM	1	1	12	3+	*HEAT*
AT-3 Sagger missile	16"/40CM–44"/110CM	1	-	19	3+	*Guided, HEAT*
7.62mm MG	16"/40CM	3	3	2	6	

The Russian BMP-1 is a useful reconnaissance vehicle. It is small and mobile, but well armed—mounting a useful 7.3cm gun and an AT-3 Sagger anti-tank missile capable of destroying any tank in existence.

In the hands of the elite *Aufklärungs Truppen*, they seek out weakness in the enemy, and lead their own troops to exploit it.

BRDM-2 AUFKLÄRUNGS ZUG

• TANK UNIT • AMPHIBIOUS • INFRA-RED (IR) • SPEARHEAD •

BRDM-2 AUFKLÄRUNGS ZUG	
4x BRDM-2	**2 POINTS**
2x BRDM-2	**1 POINTS**

COURAGE 4+	SKILL 4+
MORALE 3+	ASSAULT 6
REMOUNT 4+	COUNTERATTACK 5+

IS HIT ON 3+

FRONT	SIDE	TOP
1	0	0

TACTICAL	TERRAIN DASH	CROSS COUNTRY DASH	ROAD DASH	CROSS
10"/25CM	10"/25CM	18"/45CM	44"/110CM	4+

WEAPON	RANGE	ROF HALTED	ROF MOVING	ANTI-TANK	FIRE-POWER	NOTES
14.5mm MG	20"/50CM	3	2	5	5+	
7.62mm MG	16"/40CM	1	1	2	6	

The Soviet made BRDM-2 (*Boyevaya Razvedyvatelnaya Dozornaya Mashina 2*, or Combat Reconnaissance Patrol Vehicle 2) is a four wheel amphibious reconnaissance vehicle ideally suited for East German *Aufklärungs* troops. The vehicle has been designed to cope with a range of terrain. In addition to being amphibious, it also has two pairs of belly wheels that can be lowered by the driver for trench crossing and has a centralised tire pressure system that is used to adjust tire pressures to suit the ground conditions.

BTR-60 MOT-SCHÜTZEN BATAILLON

VOLKSARMEE

BTR-60 MOT-SCHÜTZEN BATAILLON HQ
TV111

1x MPi KM team
1x BTR-60 (TV114)

1 POINT

• INFANTRY FORMATION • HQ TRANSPORT •

COURAGE 3+	SKILL 3+
MORALE 2+	ASSAULT 5+
RALLY 3+	COUNTERATTACK 3+

IS HIT ON	INFANTRY SAVE
3+	**3+**

TACTICAL	TERRAIN DASH	CROSS COUNTRY DASH	ROAD DASH	CROSS
8"/20CM	8"/20CM	12"/30CM	12"/30CM	AUTO

WEAPON	RANGE	ROF HALTED	ROF MOVING	ANTI-TANK	FIRE-POWER	NOTES
MPi KM assault rifle team	8"/20CM	3	3	1	6	Pinned ROF 1

VOLKSARMEE

BTR-60 MOT-SCHÜTZEN KOMPANIE
TV112

VOLKSARMEE

BTR-60 MOT-SCHÜTZEN KOMPANIE
TV112

VOLKSARMEE

BTR-60 MOT-SCHÜTZEN KOMPANIE
TV112

VOLKSARMEE

T-55AM2 PANZER KOMPANIE
TV110

VOLKSARMEE

SPANDREL PANZERABWEHR ZUG
TV115

VOLKSARMEE

ZSU-23-4 SHILKA FLAK ZUG
TV120

VOLKSARMEE

2S1 CARNATION ARTILLERIE BATTERIE
TV116

VOLKSARMEE

BMP-1 AUFKLÄRUNGS ZUG
TV118

OR

VOLKSARMEE

BRDM-2 AUFKLÄRUNGS ZUG
TV119

VOLKSARMEE

SA-13 GOPHER FLAK ZUG
TV121

OR

VOLKSARMEE

SA-9 GASKIN FLAK ZUG
TV122

BTR-60 MOT-SCHÜTZEN KOMPANIE

BTR-60 MOT-SCHÜTZEN KOMPANIE

10x MPi KM team with RPG-18 anti-tank
9x RPG-7 anti-tank team
1x PKM LMG team
11x BTR-60 (TV114)　　**15 POINTS**

7x MPi KM team with RPG-18 anti-tank
6x RPG-7 anti-tank team
1x PKM LMG team
8x BTR-60 (TV114)　　**10 POINTS**

4x MPi KM team with RPG-18 anti-tank
3x RPG-7 anti-tank team
4x BTR-60 (TV114)　　**5 POINTS**

OPTIONS

- Add AGS-17 grenade launcher team & BTR-60 for +1 point.
- Add up to 2 AT-4 Spigot missile teams, each with a BTR-60, for +2 points each.
- Add SA-14 Gremlin AA missile team & BTR-60 for +1 point.

The BTR-60 Mot-Schützen Kompanie (*Motorisiertes Schützen Kompanie*, or Motorised Rifle Company) shares much of its organisation with their BMP mounted comrades. Because their BTR-60 (or *Schützenpanzerwagen-60*, SPW-60, in German) did not mount an anti-tank missile like the BMPs, a group of AT-4 Spigot anti-tank missiles on ground mounts was allocated to each company.

The SPW-60 (BTR-60) provided the majority of the armoured transport for the East German motorised riflemen. The Soviets began producing the BTR-60PB in 1966, which had a small turret armed with heavy a 14.5mm machine-gun and a co-ax 7.62mm MG. The BTR-60PB remained in production until 1976.

The BTR mounted motor riflemen make up two of the three *Motorisiertes Schützen* Regiments in each *Motorisietes Schutzen Division* (Motorised Rifle Division).

• INFANTRY UNIT •

COURAGE 4+	SKILL 4+
MORALE 3+	ASSAULT 5+
RALLY 4+	COUNTERATTACK 4+

IS HIT ON	INFANTRY SAVE
3+	**3+**

TACTICAL	TERRAIN DASH	CROSS COUNTRY DASH	ROAD DASH	CROSS
8"/20CM	8"/20CM	12"/30CM	12"/30CM	AUTO

WEAPON	RANGE	ROF HALTED	ROF MOVING	ANTI-TANK	FIRE-POWER	NOTES
MPi KM assault rifle team	8"/20CM	3	3	1	6	Pinned ROF 1
or RPG-18 anti-tank	8"/20CM	1	1	14	5+	HEAT, Slow Firing
RPG-7 anti-tank team	12"/30CM	1	1	17	4+	Assault 6, HEAT, Slow Firing
PKM LMG team	16"/40CM	7	4	2	6	Assault 6, Heavy Weapon

WEAPONS CARD

The BTR-60 Motorisiertes Schützen Kompanie is a flexible unit with a wide variety of weapons from assault rifles to automatic grenade launchers. It has an additional card, [TV113], with the data for its heavy support weapons.

WEAPON	RANGE	ROF HALTED	ROF MOVING	ANTI-TANK	FIRE-POWER	NOTES
AGS-17 grenade launcher team	16"/40CM	9	3	3	6	Assault 6, Heavy Weapon
AT-4 Spigot missile	8"/20CM - 40"/100CM	3	-	19	3+	Assault 6, Guided, HEAT, Heavy Weapon
SA-14 Gremlin AA missile team	48"/120CM	3	-	-	5+	Assault 6, Guided AA, Heavy Weapon

BTR-60 TRANSPORT

• TANK ATTACHMENT • AMPHIBIOUS • PASSENGERS 2 •

COURAGE 4+	SKILL 4+
MORALE 3+	ASSAULT 6
REMOUNT 4+	COUNTERATTACK 5+

IS HIT ON 3+		
FRONT	SIDE	TOP
1	0	0

TACTICAL	TERRAIN DASH	CROSS COUNTRY DASH	ROAD DASH	CROSS
10"/25CM	10"/25CM	16"/40CM	36"/90CM	4+

WEAPON	RANGE	ROF HALTED	ROF MOVING	ANTI-TANK	FIRE-POWER	NOTES
14.5mm MG	20"/50CM	3	2	5	5+	
7.62mm MG	16"/40CM	1	1	2	6	

Crew: 2 – driver, gunner
　　　8 Passengers
Weight: 10.3 tonnes
Length: 7.56m (24' 9.5")
Width: 2.83m (9' 3")
Height: 2.31m (7' 7")

Weapons: 14.5mm KPVT heavy machine-gun
　　　　7.62mm PKT MG
Armour: 5-10mm
Speed: 80 km/h (49.7 mph)
Range: 500 km (310 miles)

VOLKSARMEE
ZSU-23-4 SHILKA FLAK ZUG

ZSU-23-4 SHILKA FLAK ZUG

4x	ZSU-23-4 Shilka	**4 POINTS**
2x	ZSU-23-4 Shilka	**2 POINTS**

The ZSU-23-4 *Shilka* (named after a Russian river) is an effective, proven air defence artillery system mounting four liquid-cooled 23mm 2A7 cannons. The Shilka can engage targets with a fully-integrated, radar-guided, automatic target acquisition, tracking and ranging system with backup visual sights.

• TANK UNIT •

COURAGE 4+	SKILL 4+
MORALE 3+	ASSAULT 6
REMOUNT 4+	COUNTERATTACK 5+

IS HIT ON 3+		
FRONT	SIDE	TOP
👤 1	🚜 1	◼ 1

TACTICAL	TERRAIN DASH	CROSS COUNTRY DASH	ROAD DASH	CROSS
10"/25CM	14"/35CM	20"/50CM	24"/60CM	3+

WEAPON	RANGE	ROF HALTED	MOVING	ANTI-TANK	FIRE-POWER	NOTES
23mm 2A7 AA gun	20"/50CM	6	4	6	5+	*Dedicated AA, Radar*

SA-13 GOPHER FLAK ZUG

SA-13 GOPHER FLAK ZUG	
4x SA-13 Gopher	**4 POINTS**
2x SA-13 Gopher	**2 POINTS**

The SA-13 Gopher, called *Strela-10* (Arrow-10) by the Soviets, is a tracked, amphibious Surface-to-Air Missile (SAM) system. Its tracked suspension allows it to keep up with tanks in rough terrain. The missiles have both optical and infra-red guidance, with a radar system to check that the target is in range.

• TANK UNIT •

COURAGE 4+	SKILL 4+
MORALE 3+	ASSAULT -
REMOUNT 4+	COUNTERATTACK -

IS HIT ON 3+		
FRONT	SIDE	TOP
1	1	1

TACTICAL	TERRAIN DASH	CROSS COUNTRY DASH	ROAD DASH	CROSS
10"/25CM	16"/40CM	24"/60CM	28"/70CM	3+

WEAPON	RANGE	ROF HALTED	ROF MOVING	ANTI-TANK	FIRE-POWER	NOTES
SA-13 Gopher AA missile	56"/140CM	2	-	-	4+	*Guided AA*

SA-9 GASKIN FLAK ZUG

SA-13 GOPHER FLAK ZUG	
4x SA-9 Gaskin	**2 POINTS**
2x SA-9 Gaskin	**1 POINTS**

The SA-9 Gaskin (its NATO designation), called *Strela-1M* (Arrow-1M) by the Soviets, is a wheeled, amphibious Surface-to-Air Missile (SAM) system based on the same vehicle as the BRDM-2 reconnaissance vehicle. The missile system has both optical and infra-red guidance, and a target ranging radar.

• TANK UNIT • AMPHIBIOUS •

COURAGE 4+	SKILL 4+
MORALE 3+	ASSAULT -
REMOUNT 4+	COUNTERATTACK -

IS HIT ON 3+		
FRONT	SIDE	TOP
1	0	0

TACTICAL	TERRAIN DASH	CROSS COUNTRY DASH	ROAD DASH	CROSS
10"/25CM	10"/25CM	18"/45CM	44"/110CM	4+

WEAPON	RANGE	ROF HALTED	ROF MOVING	ANTI-TANK	FIRE-POWER	NOTES
SA-9 Gaskin AA missile	48"/120CM	2	-	-	5+	*Guided AA*

Crew:	3 – commander, driver, gunner	*Weapons:*	4 x 9M31M 'Strela-1M' SAM
Weight:	7 tonnes	*Armour:*	5-14mm
Length:	5.8m (19'3")	*Speed:*	100 km/h (62 mph)
Width:	2.4m (7'10")	*Engine:*	GAZ 41 V-8 water-cooled petrol
Height:	2.3m (7'6")		40 hp
	3.80m (12'6") over radar	*Range:*	750 km (315 miles)

VOLKSARMEE SUPPORT

VOLKSARMEE
2S1 CARNATION ARTILLERIE BATTERIE

2S1 CARNATION ARTILLERIE BATTERIE	
6x 2S1 Carnation	**12 POINTS**
3x 2S1 Carnation	**6 POINTS**

The 2S1 *Gvozdika* (Carnation) self-propelled howitzer is a weapon system that sharply delineates the modernisation of the Soviet artillery arm. They have gone from truck-towed howitzers to self-propelled weapons that can keep pace with tanks and infantry fighting vehicles in the new rapid-paced battle doctrine.

Armed with a 122mm 2A31 howitzer, the 2S1 is equally capable of putting rounds 15 kilometres (nearly 10 miles) down range as it is of smashing defensive positions with point-blank range direct fire. Its 22kg (48 lb) shells make short work of anti-tank missile teams, and can even penetrate a main battle tank with a square-on hit.

• TANK UNIT • AMPHIBIOUS • INFRA-RED (IR) •

COURAGE 4+	SKILL 4+
MORALE 3+	ASSAULT 6
REMOUNT 4+	COUNTERATTACK 5+

IS HIT ON 3+

FRONT	SIDE	TOP
2	1	1

TACTICAL	TERRAIN DASH	CROSS COUNTRY DASH	ROAD DASH	CROSS
10"/25CM	16"/40CM	24"/60CM	28"/70CM	3+

WEAPON	RANGE	ROF HALTED	MOVING	ANTI-TANK	FIRE-POWER	NOTES
122mm 2A31 howitzer	88"/220CM	ARTILLERY		4	3+	*Smoke Bombardment*
or Direct fire	24"/60CM	1	1	21	2+	*Brutal, HEAT, Slow Firing, Smoke*

Crew: 4 - commander, gunner, loader, driver
Weight: 16 tonnes
Length: 7.26m (23' 10")
Width: 2.85m (9' 4")
Height: 2.73m (8' 11")

Weapons: 122mm 2A31 howitzer
Armour: 20mm
Speed: 640km/h (37 mph)
Engine: YaMZ-238N diesel 220 kW (300 hp)
Range: 500 km (310 miles)

VOLKSARMEE
BM-21 HAIL RAKETENWERFER BATTERIE

BM-21 HAIL RAKETENWERFER BATTERIE	
6x BM-21 Hail	**10 POINTS**
3x BM-21 Hail	**5 POINTS**

The BM-21 *Grad* (Hail) is a direct descendant for the famous *Katyusha* rocket launcher of the Second World War. The box launcher housing four rows of ten tubes is mounted on a Ural 6x6 truck. The BM-21 can fire fin-stabilised 122mm rockets, which can have fragmentation, chemical, or incendiary warheads, up to 16 kilometres (10 miles).

• UNARMOURED TANK UNIT •

COURAGE 4+	SKILL 4+
MORALE 3+	ASSAULT -
RALLY 4+	COUNTERATTACK -

IS HIT ON	TANK SAVE
3+	**5+**

TACTICAL	TERRAIN DASH	CROSS COUNTRY DASH	ROAD DASH	CROSS
8"/20CM	8"/20CM	14"/35CM	36"/90CM	4+

WEAPON	RANGE	ROF HALTED	MOVING	ANTI-TANK	FIRE-POWER	NOTES
BM-21 rocket launcher	96"/240CM	SALVO		3	4+	*Smoke Bombardment*

Crew: 5 - commander, gunner, 2x loaders, driver
Weight: 14 tonnes
Length: 7.35m (24' 1")
Width: 2.40m (7 ft 10 in)
Height: 3.09m (10 ft 2 in)
Weapons: 122mm 2B5 40-barrelled rocket launcher
Speed: 75 km/h (47 mph)
Engine: ZiL-375 V8 gasoline 130 kW (180 hp)

VOLKSARMEE
BMP-1 OBSERVATION POST

OBSERVATION POST

1x BMP-1 OP **1 POINT**

You must field either:

- *a Volksarmee 2S1 Carnation Artillerie Batterie* (TV116), *or*
- *a Volksarmee BM-21 Hail Raketen Batterie* (TV117)

before you may field a BMP-1 OP.

Artillery observers operate well forward with the lead battalions, so they need an armoured vehicle with space for additional radios. The BMP also looks like a conventional infantry fighting vehicle, making it less obvious to the enemy.

• INDEPENDENT TANK UNIT • AMPHIBIOUS • INFRA-RED (IR) • OBSERVER • SCOUT •

COURAGE 4+	SKILL 4+
MORALE 3+	ASSAULT 6
REMOUNT 4+	COUNTERATTACK 5+

IS HIT ON 3+

FRONT	SIDE	TOP
2	2	1

TACTICAL	TERRAIN DASH	CROSS COUNTRY DASH	ROAD DASH	CROSS
10"/25CM	16"/40CM	28"/70CM	32"/80CM	3+

WEAPON	RANGE	ROF HALTED	ROF MOVING	ANTI-TANK	FIRE-POWER	NOTES
7.62mm MG	16"/40CM	3	3	2	6	

VOLKSARMEE
SPANDREL PANZERABWEHR ZUG

SPANDREL PANZERABWEHR ZUG

3x Spandrel **2 POINTS**
2x Spandrel **1 POINTS**

The *9P148 Konkurs* (Contest, or Spandrel as its missile is designated by NATO) is a light mobile armoured vehicle mounting five excellent wire-guided *9M113 Konkurs* (AT-5 Spandrel) anti-tank missiles. The 9P148 vehicle is based on the same vehicle used in the reconnaissance role as the BRDM-2. It has good cross-country and road speed allowing it to get into good positions from which to launch its missiles.

• TANK UNIT • AMPHIBIOUS • INFRA-RED (IR) •

COURAGE 4+	SKILL 4+
MORALE 3+	ASSAULT 6
REMOUNT 4+	COUNTERATTACK 6

IS HIT ON 3+

FRONT	SIDE	TOP
1	0	0

TACTICAL	TERRAIN DASH	CROSS COUNTRY DASH	ROAD DASH	CROSS
10"/25CM	10"/25CM	18"/45CM	44"/110CM	4+

WEAPON	RANGE	ROF HALTED	ROF MOVING	ANTI-TANK	FIRE-POWER	NOTES
AT-5 Spandrel missile	8"/20CM– 48"/120CM	1	-	21	3+	*Guided, HEAT*

MI-24 HIND BATTLE HELICOPTER SQUADRON
VOLKSARMEE

MI-24 HIND BATTLE HELICOPTER SQUADRON

4x Mi-24 Hind	**12 POINTS**
2x Mi-24 Hind	**6 POINTS**

If a force contains an Mi-24 Hind Battle Helicopter Squadron, it may also take an Mi-24 Hind Assault Landing company (TV124). The Assault Landing company must not exceed the combined Passenger Capacity of the Mi-24 Hind Battle Helicopter Squadron.

• HELICOPTER AIRCRAFT UNIT • PASSENGERS 2 •

COURAGE 4+	SKILL 4+
MORALE 3+	

IS HIT ON	AIRCRAFT SAVE
3+	**4+**

TACTICAL	TERRAIN DASH	CROSS COUNTRY DASH	ROAD DASH	CROSS
UNLIMITED				AUTO

WEAPON	RANGE	ROF HALTED	ROF MOVING	ANTI-TANK	FIRE-POWER	NOTES
AT-6 Spiral missile	8"/20CM–20"/50CM	-	1	23	3+	Guided, HEAT
12.7mm Yak-B Gatling gun	8"/20CM	-	3	5	5+	Anti-helicopter
57mm UB-32 rocket launcher	20"/50CM	SALVO		3	6	One Shot

Unlike Western attack helicopters, which play hide and seek with their opponents, the tactics of the Mil Mi-24D Hind, called rather appropriately the *Krokodil* (Crocodile) by its crews, are more aggressive. These large, armoured assault helicopters close with the enemy, firing all the way with their four-barrelled 12.7mm YakB Gatling guns and UB-32 57mm rocket pods, or AT-6 Spiral, *Shturm* (Storm) to the gunner firing them, anti-tank guided missiles. The Mi-24 can also transport a small squad of troops, giving Soviet commanders great flexibility. The helicopters saturate the objective with fire, then swoop in and deliver the infantry to hold the position.

Crew: 2 – pilot, gunner
Weight: 12 tonnes
Length: 17.50m (57' 5")
Rotor: 17.3m (56' 7")
Armour: stops 12.7mm rounds
Speed: 335 km/h (208 mph)

SU-25 FROGFOOT AVIATION COMPANY

Red Banner support options are the units that are in Team Yankee. The cards for these units are packed in their boxes.

SU-25 FROGFOOT AVIATION COMPANY	
6x SU-25 Frogfoot	**21 POINTS**
4x SU-25 Frogfoot	**14 POINTS**
2x SU-25 Frogfoot	**7 POINTS**

The Sukhoi Su-25 Frogfoot, known to its crew as the *Grach* (Rook), is the Soviets' modern-day equivalent of the legendary Il-2 *Shturmovik* of the Second World War. It's tough and sturdy, able to sustain multiple hits and still bring its pilot home. Flying low and slow, it can safely attack enemy troops in close proximity to its own.

The SU-25 carries an impressive array of weaponry, including air-to-surface missiles and unguided rockets, on its ten under-wing hardpoints, as well as having a twin-barrelled

• STRIKE AIRCRAFT UNIT •

COURAGE 4+	SKILL 5+
MORALE 3+	

IS HIT ON	AIRCRAFT SAVE
3+	4+

TACTICAL	TERRAIN DASH	CROSS COUNTRY DASH	ROAD DASH	CROSS
UNLIMITED				AUTO

WEAPON	RANGE	ROF HALTED	ROF MOVING	ANTI-TANK	FIRE-POWER	NOTES
Kh-25 air-ground missile	8"/20CM–28"/70CM	-	1	27	2+	*Brutal, Guided, HEAT*
30mm GSh-30-2 gun	8"/20CM	-	3	7	5+	*Anti-helicopter*
57mm UB-32 rocket launcher	20"/50CM	SALVO		3	6	*One Shot*

GSh-30-2 30mm cannon in the nose. It is the ideal aircraft to support the Warsaw Pact's tank and motor rifle divisions.

Crew:	1 - pilot	Weapon:	30mm GSh-301 cannon
Empty:	10 tonnes	Armour:	Titanium bathtub
Loaded:	15 tonnes	Speed:	975 km/h (606 mph)
Length:	15.53m (51')	Engines:	2 × R-195 turbojets,
Wingspan:	14.36m (48')		44 kN (9,921 lbf) thrust
Wing area:	33.7m² (323 ft²)	Range:	750 km (465 miles)

VOLKSARMEE

MI-24 HIND ASSAULT LANDING COMPANY

MI-24 HIND ASSAULT LANDING COMPANY	
4x MPi KM team with RPG-18 anti-tank	
4x RPG-7 anti-tank team	**3 POINTS**
2x MPi KM team with RPG-18 anti-tank	
2x RPG-7 anti-tank team	**1 POINTS**

Your force must contain an Mi-24 Hind Battle Helicopter Squadron (TV123) to take an Mi-24 Hind Assault Landing company.

• INFANTRY ATTACHMENT •

COURAGE 4+	SKILL 4+
MORALE 3+	ASSAULT 5+
RALLY 4+	COUNTERATTACK 4+

IS HIT ON	INFANTRY SAVE
3+	3+

TACTICAL	TERRAIN DASH	CROSS COUNTRY DASH	ROAD DASH	CROSS
8"/20CM	8"/20CM	12"/30CM	12"/30CM	AUTO

WEAPON	RANGE	ROF HALTED	ROF MOVING	ANTI-TANK	FIRE-POWER	NOTES
MPi KM assault rifle team or RPG-18 anti-tank	8"/20CM 8"/20CM	3 1	3 1	1 14	6 5+	*Pinned ROF 1* *HEAT, Slow Firing*
RPG-7 anti-tank team	12"/30CM	1	1	17	4+	*Assault 6, HEAT, Slow Firing*

VOLKSARMEE

PAINTING VOLKSARMEE

GERMAN ARMOUR - OLIVE DRAB

T-55AM2
3 COLOUR CAMO

T-72
PLAIN GREEN

In the late 80's the Volksarmee changed from an all-over green scheme to a 3 colour camo scheme. We chose to use this scheme on our studio army because it's just cool. Alternatively you can paint East German tanks in a plain green scheme using either NATO green or Soviet Green.

SOVIET AIRCRAFT

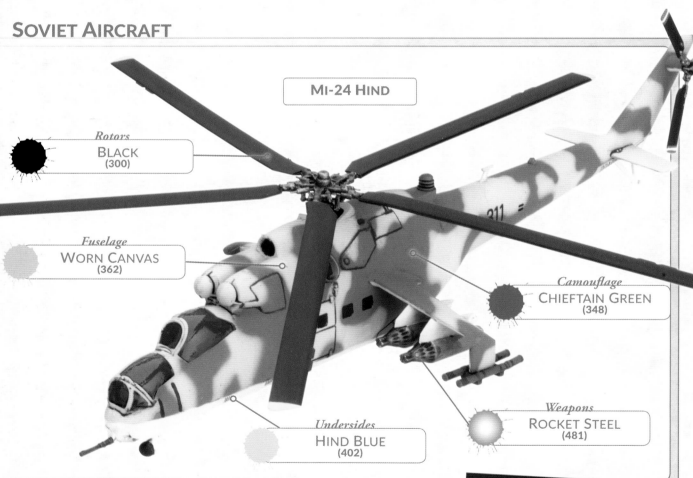

MI-24 HIND

Rotors
BLACK
(300)

Fuselage
WORN CANVAS
(362)

Camouflage
CHIEFTAIN GREEN
(348)

Undersides
HIND BLUE
(402)

Weapons
ROCKET STEEL
(481)

This painting guide uses the *Colours Of War* painting system.

The *Colours of War* book is a detailed and comprehensive guide to painting miniatures that shows you, step-by-step, everything you need to know to field beautifully-painted miniatures in your *Team Yankee* games. While *Colours of War* focuses on the Second World War miniatures of *Flames Of War*, the techniques work just the same for *Team Yankee*.

Visit the *Team Yankee* website: www.Team-Yankee.com for more information.

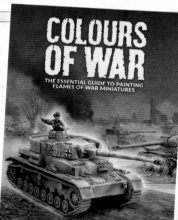

COLOURS OF WAR

THE ESSENTIAL GUIDE TO PAINTING
FLAMES OF WAR MINIATURES

VOLKSARMEE 3-COLOUR CAMOUFLAGE

COLOUR PALETTE

NATO GREEN
(341)

WORN RUBBER
(302)

HARRIER GREY
(304)

DRY DUST
(364)

BATTLEFIELD BROWN
(324)

ORDNANCE SHADE
(492)

East German vehicles can be painted following the Soviet painting guide on page 116 of the *Team Yankee* rulebook using Soviet Green.

If you want a brighter green you can use this painting guide but skip the Worn Rubber and Harrier Grey steps. This is what we did on the T-72 on the previous page.

There were few guidelines for applying the camouflage. The stripes should be painted at an angle of 30 to 60 degrees, which had to adhere to the vehicle edge. No camouflage was applied to the wheels to avoid striking colour change while driving.

NATO GREEN
Large Brush

BASECOAT *your tank with NATO Green. Two thin coats are preferable to one thick coat. Alternatively you can use a NATO Green spray can for your undercoat.*

WORN RUBBER
Large Brush

PAINT *Patches of Worn Rubber. These are painted in an irregular pattern, but should be at 60° to the vertical.*

HARRIER GREY
Large Brush

PAINT *Patches of Harrier Grey in a similar way to the Worn Rubber.*

DRY DUST
Large Drybrush

DRYBRUSH *the tank with Dry Dust, concentrating on edges, raised details, and upper surfaces to add highlights.*

BATTLEFIELD BROWN
Large Brush

BASECOAT *your tracks with Battlefield Brown. Keep the tracks separate to make them easier to paint. Remember that the top of the track will be hidden by the track guards.*

ORDNANCE SHADE
Small Brush

WASH *the tracks with Ordnance Shade.*

DRY DUST
Small Drybrush

DRYBRUSH *the lower areas of the tank, concentrating on the flat surfaces, to give the effect of heavy dry dust.*

Adding decals before drybrushing the Dry Dust will help give it the 'painted-on' look

ORDNANCE SHADE
Small Brush

TARGET WASH *the details with Ordnance Shade to add definition to the vehicle. You may find it easier to apply your target wash if you give the vehicle a coat of gloss varnish first.*

Be sure to visit **WWW.TEAM-YANKEE.COM** for more in-depth painting articles and videos.

WEATHERING PLAIN GREEN

COLOUR PALETTE

SPLINTER GREEN
(343)

GREASE BROWN
(320)

COMRADE KHAKI
(326)

RUST ORANGE
(360)

MOTHERLAND EARTH
(383)

DRY DUST
(364)

Here are a few tips for adding depth to Soviet armour to make them stand out on the battlefield.

Be careful to build the weathering up carefully, to avoid overdoing it.

SPLINTER GREEN — *Medium Brush*

PAINT *chips and scratches with a fine brush, concentrating on edges and areas of heavy use.*

GREASE BROWN — *Fine Brush*

FILL IN *the centre of the chips with Grease Brown, leaving the edges of the Splinter Green Showing.*

GREASE BROWN — *Fine Brush*

PAINT *vertical streaks with very thinned down Grease Brown, starting at corrosion points like paint chips and weld lines.*

COMRADE KHAKI — *Fine Brush*

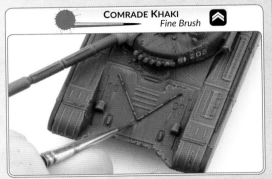

BUILD UP *the streaks with thinned down Comrade Khaki, Rust Orange or Motherland Earth.*

COMRADE KHAKI — *Fine Brush*

TARGET WASH *weld lines with Comrade Khaki. Be careful not to go too overboard with this; 'less is more'. Painting a gloss varnish first will help with your paint flow.*

DRY DUST — *Small Drybrush*

DRYBRUSH *Dry Dust on to your vehicle, brushing vertical streaks up and down to represent rain-streaked dust.*

WARSAW PACT TANK CREW

COLOUR PALETTE

COMRADE KHAKI
(326)

LUFTWAFFE BLUE
(401)

ORDNANCE SHADE
(493)

WORN CANVAS
(306)

COMRADE KHAKI — *Large Brush*
LUFTWAFFE BLUE — *Large Brush*

BASECOAT *the uniform Luftwaffe Blue and the helmet Comrade Khaki.*

ORDNANCE SHADE — *Large Brush*

WASH *the helmet and overalls with Ordnance Shade. You can substitute Black heavily thinned with water.*

50% COMRADE KHAKI 50% WORN CANVAS — *Medium Brush*
LUFTWAFFE BLUE — *Medium Brush*

HIGHLIGHT *the helmet with a mix of Comrade Khaki and Worn Canvas. Tidy up the overalls with Luftwaffe Blue.*

EAST GERMAN UNIFORMS

COLOUR PALETTE

BATTLEDRESS BROWN
(325)

ORDNANCE SHADE
(493)

WOOL BROWN
(328)

The East German uniforms had a subtle camouflage pattern.

From a distance the camouflage pattern blends into the rest of the uniform, so don't feel as though you have to paint it.

BATTLEDRESS BROWN *Large Brush*

BASECOAT *the uniform Battledress Brown, using two thin coats if necessary to achieve an even coverage.*

ORDNANCE SHADE *Large Brush*

WASH *the figure liberally with Ordnance Shade to add depth to the uniform.*

BATTLEDRESS BROWN *Medium Brush*

TIDY UP *the uniform with Battledress Brown, leaving dark shadows in the recessed areas.*

WOOL BROWN *Fine Brush*

ACTUAL SIZE

HIGHLIGHT *the edges and raised folds of the uniform with Wool Brown.*

EAST GERMAN CAMOUFLAGE

COLOUR PALETTE

WOOL BROWN
(328)

ORDNANCE SHADE
(493)

DARK LEATHER
(322)

If you want to attempt to paint the camouflage, start with a lighter colour and add dark brown vertical stripes.

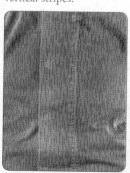

WOOL BROWN *Medium Brush*

BASECOAT *the uniform Wool Brown, using two thin coats if necessary to achieve an even coverage.*

ORDNANCE SHADE *Fine Brush*

WASH *the figure liberally with Ordnance Shade to add depth to the uniform.*

WOOL BROWN *Fine Brush*

TIDY UP *the uniform with Wool Brown, leaving dark shadows in the recessed areas.*

DARK LEATHER *Fine Brush*

ACTUAL SIZE

PAINT *vertical streaks on the uniform. The thinner and closer together the streaks are the more accurate the uniform will look.*

Webbing Equipment

Colour Palette			

COMRADE KHAKI (326)

ORDNANCE SHADE (492)

MILITARY KHAKI (327)

COMRADE KHAKI
Medium Brush

ORDNANCE SHADE
Fine Brush

MILITARY KHAKI
Fine Brush

ACTUAL SIZE

BLOCK PAINT *the webbing with Comrade Khaki.*

WASH *the details carefully with Ordnance Shade.*

HIGHLIGHT *with Military Khaki.*

MPi KM & RPK Assault Rifles

Colour Palette			

BATTLEFIELD BROWN (324)

DARK GUNMETAL (480)

ORDNANCE SHADE (492)

**BATTLEFIELD BROWN
DARK GUNMETAL**
Medium Brush

ORDNANCE SHADE
Fine Brush

BATTLEFIELD BROWN
Fine Brush

ACTUAL SIZE

PAINT *the rifles Battlefield Brown and Dark Gunmetal.*

WASH *the whole rifle with Ordnance Shade.*

HIGHLIGHT *the wooden rifle parts with Battlefield Brown.*

Basing East German Infantry

*Formation Commander
MPi KM assault rifle team*

Base the Commander on a small base
with a radio operator and rifleman.

MPi KM assault rifle team with RPG-18 anti-tank

Base an MPi KM assault rifle team on a medium base. Teams combine a machine-gunner armed with an RPK squad automatic weapon and three riflemen armed with MPi KM rifles and RPG-18 anti-tank weapons.

Unit Leaders replace the two MPi KM riflemen with an officer and radio operator.

Some players like to mark their Unit Leaders with a small piece of terrain on the base or a dot of paint on the back of the stand for easy identification.

*AGS-17
grenade launcher team*

*PKM
LMG*

*SA-14
Gremlin*

*AT-4
Spigot*

Weapons teams

Base Weapons teams on a large base with three heavy weapons
(AGS-17 grenade launchers, PKM LMGs, SA-14 Gremlins, or AT-4 Spigots)
and three rifle-armed assistants.

RPG-7 anti-tank team

Base an RPG-7 anti-tank team on a small base,
with one miniature armed with an RPG-7,
and a rifle armed assistant.

BBC Television Nine O'Clock News, Tim Mannering reporting, Lingen 11 August:

"I'm standing here in the street of the Lower Saxon town of Lingen, on the Dortmund-Ems Canal. As you can see, a stream of military traffic is heading west along the B213 road. As far as I can tell, these are Dutch troops, though there are some West Germans too."

The reporter catches the attention of a Dutch soldier walking pass. "Sir, are you withdrawing?"

"Those Russians just keep coming, just when you think you're safe, then the East Germans attack." He waves off the reporter before hopping on a passing armoured vehicle.

A jet then roars overhead and the reporter ducks before the camera lowers and the transmission ends.

Volksarmee Radio (former DLF radio station), Uelzen, 13 August

"...stay in your homes and remain calm. The People's Army has liberated you from the capitalist boot. Your future is secure in the warm embrace of the workers paradise. The German Democratic Republic has the best interests of the German people at heart and your freedoms are not threatened. Please cooperate with our soldiers and officials.

Please stay in..."

CNN News Report, 13 August:

"Breaking tonight, Warsaw Pact troops have crossed into The Netherlands and are fighting their way south towards the Belgian border. Fighting is fierce around the towns of Almelo and Rijssen as Dutch troops fight to hold off Soviet and East German attackers."

Allgemeiner Deutscher Nachrichtendienst, East Berlin, 14 August:

"9. Panzer Division, fighting alongside the Soviet 20th Guards Army, have swept through The Netherlands, brushing all resistance aside. Our mighty Volksarmee troops have proven themselves some of the best fighting troops in the Warsaw Pact. They now stand in the town of Arnhem, across the river from them are newly arrived British troops. Will the British once more taste defeat at the hands of Germans forces as they did almost 41 years earlier?"

NATO AND WARSAW PACT DEPLOYMENT AND PLANNED WARSAW PACT ATTACKS

THE COLD WAR

Kiel

Rosto

Lübeck

Wilhelmshaven

Bremerhaven

Hamburg

LANDJUT
xxxx
NORTHAG

1ST
**NETHERLANDS
CORPS**

2ND
**GUARD
TANK
ARM**

Bremen

xxx

1ST
**GERMAN
CORPS**

THE
NETHERLANDS

Hannover

1ST
**BRITISH
CORPS**

3RD
**SHOCK
ARMY**

xxx

3RD US CORPS

Magdeburg

1ST
**BELGIUM
CORPS**

EAS

3RD
**FRENCH
CORPS**

Essen

**GROUP OF
SOVIET FORCE
IN GERMANY
(GSFG)**

Düsseldorf

NORTHAG
xxxx
CENTAG

3RD
**GERMAN
CORPS**

Cologne

Leipzig

8TH
**GUARDS
ARMY**

BONN

xxx

5TH
US CORPS

Fulda

Frankfurt

xxx

**WEST
GERMANY**

Rhine River

Saarbrücken

7TH
US CORPS

Nürnberg

FRANCE

CENTAG
xxxx
SOUTHAG

1ST
**FRENCH
CORPS**

Stuttgart

2ND
**GERMAN
CORPS**

2ND
**FRENCH
CORPS**

Danube River

Munich